Been There, Done That, Doing It Better!

Been There, Done That, Doing It Better!

A Witty Look at Growing Older by a Formerly Young Person

Natasha Josefowitz, PhD

Blue Mountain Press™
Boulder, Colorado

Dedication

To my ever-supportive husband, Herman Gadon,
who has inspired the direction of my life
and with whom I am trying to age both
with philosophy and good humor.

Acknowledgments

My first acknowledgment goes to Patti Wayant, my editor, on this, our fourth book together. I appreciate as always her input from her own poetic soul and life experiences.

To Erika Pfeiffer, my secretary, who not only has typed and retyped the poems but has contributed significantly both grammatically and in the sharpening of ideas.

I also want to thank the residents of the White Sands of La Jolla, my new retirement community, for having endured during early morning breakfasts the recitations of my poems with suggestions on what to include, improve, or reject.

Library of Congress Catalog Card Number: 2009016283
ISBN: 978-1-59842-423-2

█ and Blue Mountain Press are registered in U.S. Patent and Trademark Office.
Certain trademarks are used under license.

Printed in China.
First Printing: 2009

✪ This book is printed on recycled paper.

This book is printed on archival quality, white felt, 110 lb. paper. This paper has been specially produced to be acid free (neutral pH) and contains no groundwood or unbleached pulp. It conforms with the requirements of the American National Standards Institute, Inc., so as to ensure that this book will last and be enjoyed by future generations.

Library of Congress Cataloging-in-Publication Data

Josefowitz, Natasha.
  Been there, done that, doing it better! : a witty look at growing older by a formerly young person / Natasha Josefowitz.
     p. cm.
  ISBN 978-1-59842-423-2 (trade pbk. : alk. paper) 1. Aging. I. Title.
  HQ1061.J675 2009
  305.26—dc22
                                                2009016283

Blue Mountain Arts, Inc.
P.O. Box 4549, Boulder, Colorado 80306

Contents

Been There, Done That...

*W*e've been there
done that —
mostly good things
but also mistakes
We've traveled the world
met interesting people
and boring ones
had conversations
that were meaningful
and some best forgotten
We've read books
that changed our lives
walked out of bad movies
danced on tabletops
dreamt big dreams
failed at times
thought a lot
wrote some
exercised too little
had kids and grandkids
inspired some people
offended others
loved well
and grieved losses
We've known good health
and illness
the highs and the lows
We've been there
done that —
and learned a lot on the way
So now
we're doing it better

This Isn't So Bad

There is less ambivalence
than I expected
about growing older
and more pleasure
than anticipated
Not only isn't it
as bad as all that
it's even pretty good
And so we all need to celebrate
our accumulated years
for the growing wisdom
they are providing us

It's the Metallic Age

Silver in our hair
gold in our teeth
titanium implants in our hips
steel pins in our knees
metal rods in our spines
lead in our feet
and a platinum card in our pockets

Getting There Is All the Fun!

I always tried to do it all
to become a better person
to acquire the sufficient knowledge
the necessary skills
the right attitude

And when I accomplished it
finally made it
or knew just about enough
to feel I had arrived
I set my eyes again
on some new, distant goal
working hard
to get to that next
arrival place

Now I have come to realize
that it is not the destination
that matters
but the journey

Good Enough

I've been a good-enough parent —
could have been better
but the kids grew up okay

I've been a good-enough wife —
could have been more attentive
but the marriage has lasted

I've been a good-enough daughter —
could have been more understanding
but my parents and I loved one another

I could have been a more available friend
but my friends are sticking by me

I could have been a more serious student
but managed to learn what I needed

I could have been a more committed teacher
but was able to inspire a few students

I could have been a better person
but I have been good enough

$\mathcal{W}$e are
the re-invented generation
the re-wired
the re-tired
with new tires
ready to keep rolling
We are the geri-actives
the wise old-timers
We're not only senior citizens
we're seasoned citizens
It's when you get over the hill
that you can start to pick up speed

Body Shops

When I begin to
nickel-and-dime an old car
when the gasket needs replacement
or the hoses become brittle
or the motor needs a tune-up
when I begin to spend
a lot of money on my old car
and it sits in the repair shop
more often than at home
I think it's time to get a new model

When I begin to nickel-and-dime myself
when small things start going wrong
like eyesight or hearing
when hair thins out
and skin gets dry
when walking is less brisk
and I pant at the top
of the second flight of stairs
when getting out
of a deep armchair
becomes a challenge
I'm ready for a new model, too

But while cars have body shops
bodies don't have shops
and while I can turn in
an old car for a newer one
I cannot turn in a 1926 body
for a newer design
So I keep fixing the old model
hoping it will keep running
more or less smoothly
for another few years

Past Middle Age

I always thought of myself
as middle-aged
until I realized that
it is my children
who are middle-aged

It's only when my children
will be a lot "older"
and will start having gray hair
that I will be ready
to be "old!"

My Frontal
Lobe Is
Shrinking

My frontal lobe is shrinking
It's the seat of impulse control
My frontal lobe is shrinking
So I ask embarrassing questions
or drone on about irrelevant topics
My frontal lobe is shrinking
due to the aging process
You'll just have to put up with me

Tempus Fugit

Immersed in the moment
I already regret the leaving
even before I have left

Trying to stay in the present
I anticipate
the end before it has ended

And so I am sad
for the joy
that won't last

Who Is That Old Woman in the Mirror?

Every morning when I wake up
I brush my teeth
and look in the mirror

Every morning when I get up
I am surprised
at what is reflected in that mirror

Every morning I expect
to see a youngish face
and every morning what is there
is a rather oldish face
with more wrinkles
than I last remembered
and grayer hair than
I saw yesterday

Every morning as I brush my teeth
I shake my head in disbelief

The Hearing Aid

I say "What?" a lot
When people tell me something
I say
"What did you say?"
and "Can you say that again?"
"What?"
I didn't hear you
Speak louder
You're mumbling
Please repeat

So I got a hearing aid
In the daytime
I kept it in my purse
and in the evening
in a drawer
It didn't help
Then my husband got one, too
So now when he says "What?"
I say
"Is your hearing aid on?"
"You should wear your hearing aid"
"Why don't you use your hearing aid?"
And he says
"What did you say?"

Have You Noticed?

The world is changing
They build the stairs steeper
bookshelves higher, the streets longer
and everything is farther away

Have you noticed
that newsprint is getting smaller
that everyone has begun to mumble
or whisper all the time

Also, people are much younger today
than I was at the same age
yet people my age are older than I am
I ran into an old friend of mine
and he had aged so much
he did not recognize me

Numbers are also being changed
clothes that used to be labeled an 8
now have tags that say 14
and bathroom scales show
higher numbers than ever before
Yes, the world is changing
and not for the better

Food splatters more than it used to
wine glasses are easier to tip over
grocery bags are heavier
books take longer to read
parking spaces are scarcer
lines at the movies are longer
The weather is changing, too
It's colder in the winter
and hotter in the summer

Have you noticed all this?

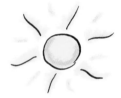

The Problem
with 20/20 Vision

He had a cataract removed
and when he came home
he was surprised
that he had aged
ten years in two days
"Look at all my wrinkles," he said
and I replied
"You better not look at me"

New Glasses

I just found out
something unpleasant
about myself
I am vain
I did not know this
until at age eighty
I got my first pair of glasses
I had needed reading glasses
but not for distance
not for all-day wear
and now that I need glasses
I don't like
the way I look
remembering that
boys don't make passes
at girls who wear glasses
and indeed this past month
while I was wearing
my new glasses
no boys made any passes
not that anyone did before
but now I can attribute
this lack of attention
to those
new spectacles
on my nose

Change of Wardrobe

I used to be thin
I wore very tight jeans
waist-cinching belts
and form-fitting clothes
When I used to be thin
I showed off my figure

Now that I have a matronly shape
I wear boxy jackets that go over my hips

Now that I have a full, mature body
I wear loose dresses to hide my stomach

Now that I've gone from size 8 to 14
I don't tuck in my blouses
but wear them over pants

But in order to ward off osteoporosis
we need to be weight bearing
which I am all day long

And so now that I weigh
a few pounds too many
I eat what I want
and say to hell with it all

Sometimes I Forget

Sometimes
when I dial a phone number
by the time someone answers
I forget whom it was I was calling

Sometimes
when I write a note to myself
to answer a call or a letter
I forget where I put it

Sometimes when I leave the house
I forget whether I left the lights on
or turned the stove off

Sometimes
I have to check if my toothbrush is wet
to know whether I had already
brushed my teeth that morning

Sometimes on my way home
I drive right by my house
and only notice it a few blocks later

Sometimes
I forget whether I meant to say something
or whether I have already said it

But often
I remember the kind words
the sweet smells
sunlit days
a tender touch
a book I loved
music, a picture
a special event

I guess I remember more than I forget

Little Pieces of Paper

Little pieces of paper
clutter my life
A hurriedly noted
phone number, whose?
An address, why?
A disembodied name
not connected
to anyone I know
Little pieces of paper
all over my desk
on the kitchen counter
by my bedside
to remind me of
something
to help me remember
someone
who had called
to invite me
to go somewhere
or to cancel something
or to announce
an important event

So now I won't show up
when I should
or I'll arrive
when I'm not expected
I won't reply
or I'll forget to call or do something
I will be remiss
and then chastised
and made to feel guilty
all because of
these little pieces
of paper
all over the house

Good Intentions

Before going on vacation
I promised myself
to exercise a lot
and eat very little
but somehow
I got confused
and ended up
doing just the opposite

Choices

It's Always Too Little or Too Much

When I'm home doing nothing
I wish I were out doing something —
something exciting, of course

When I'm off doing something
and I'm harried and pressured
I wish I were home
doing nothing

To not decide is also making a choice
and a mistake is just another
necessary learning experience

My To-Do List

$\mathcal{M}$y to-do list is on my desk
I seem to keep adding more things to it
than checking things off as "done"

It starts with
    return sweater
    find receipt for sweater
    read book lent by a friend
    remember the name of that friend
    call sick cousin before she gets well

And goes on with
    organize organizer
    put photos from ten years ago in album
    learn how to program cell phone
    find instruction booklet
    update address book
    go through sock drawer and remove unmatched ones
    throw out last year's travel brochures
    plan weekend away for when we have time

And ends with
    today — go to a movie
    tomorrow — start working on list

Slow Down

I need to slow down
chat with my neighbor
look at a flower
read a book
that has nothing to do
with personal growth

I need to slow down
call up a friend
smile at a child
go to a movie
read a magazine
that will teach me
absolutely nothing

I need to slow down
take a walk
watch a sunset
take an art class

I need to slow down

Death and Taxes

They say that there are
only two things that are
inevitable: death and taxes
Yet there are many more things
that are predictable
We will also experience losses —
losing people we love —
endure sickness
financial problems
live through tragedies
emotional upheavals
and if we're lucky
we will live long enough
to lose youth and vigor
and face the disabilities of old age
none of which we can control
But what we can do
is choose how to respond
We can choose optimism
instead of giving in
and strength and courage
instead of giving up
find humor in our foibles
and forgiveness for the frailties of others
Death and taxes may be inevitable
but how we respond to life is not

It's Not Too Late...

No one has ever wished
on his deathbed
that he had worked harder
or owned more things
or had more power

Instead
there is often a longing
for having spent more time with family
and having loved better

It is not too late
to change our priorities

You Decide

He: Would you like to go out for dinner tonight?

She: Great idea, where shall we go?

He: You choose

She: Oh, I don't know, you decide

He: How about French?

She: No, it's too rich

He: Italian?

She: No, I don't feel like pasta, something lighter

He: How about Asian?

She: No, it's always too spicy

He: Mexican?

She: No, it's too greasy

He: Okay, how about fast food?

She: You've got to be kidding

He: I tell you what, let's have a bite at home
        and go to a movie
She: Great idea
He: What would you like to see?
She: Nothing scary
He: Okay
She: Nothing too sad
He: Okay
She: Let's go to a neighborhood movie
He: Okay
She: Something that doesn't end too late
He: Okay
She: So, you choose
He: Let's just stay home and rent a movie
She: Great idea
He: What would you like to see?
She: You decide

The Morning Walk

The path has stones
unevenly placed
I'm careful not to turn my ankle
The path has grass
that is still wet from dew
I'm careful not to slip
as I walk on the path with my dog
every morning
before breakfast

On paved streets
people pass
without noticing each other
On a dirt path
people say hello
or at least nod
in recognition
that there are fewer of us there
who walk without a destination

Paved streets
are lined with buildings
doors to apartments
windows into storefronts
The path is lined with trees
and the backyards of homes
with disintegrating fences

It's cold in the morning
before breakfast
and I hurry my step
to get to the end of the path
so I can turn around
and go home to a cup of hot tea

From Pack Rat to Minimalist

I want to go
from being possessed by possessions
to bare necessities

From:
just in case I might need it
or it may become fashionable again someday
or it reminds me of that trip
or a friend gave it to me
or I loved that book
or I may read through that stack of articles
when I have time

To:
the school south of the border
the homeless shelter
the trash

I dream of empty shelves and empty drawers
of photos neatly placed in albums
of files organized and updated
I dream of closets coordinated by color
with clothes not scrunched together
getting wrinkled
of sweaters neatly stacked
of toiletries not overrunning
all the available space by the sink

I dream of a kitchen
where I can find what I need
and not search for it
in ten different places
of a garage devoid of
discarded cardboard boxes
rusted garden tools
and broken suitcases

I dream of having looked
through all those videotapes
so I can throw them out
getting rid of that half-knitted sweater
I will never finish
and those clothes two sizes smaller
than I can wear now
I will give up the hope
of getting thinner
give up the hope
of having more time
in some not-too-distant future
and still believe
that from pack rat
I can become
a minimalist
someday

Lessons
Learned

Gifts

Give your children
more of your presence
instead of more presents

When I was young
I used to wonder
what I would be
when I grew up

And now
that I am all grown up
I do not wonder
what I will be
for I have found out
who I am

Be Kinder Than Necessary

Be kinder than necessary
for everyone is fighting
some type of battle
Do an unexpected
act of kindness
It may help someone
through his or her day
Extend a hand
when not required
Smile at someone
who's looking sad
Sit next to a person
who seems lonely
Make someone laugh
with a funny tale
Wave at the stranger
crossing your path
Hug the friend
who's just standing there
Do an unexpected
act of kindness
It just may help
someone get through
his or her day

If...

If you look
but you do not see...

If you listen
but you do not hear...

If you talk
but you do not think...

If you touch
but you do not feel...

Then you exist
but you do not live

Please Consider

Just as not everything worth doing
is worth doing well
not everything worth having
is worth paying
a price for

Eat Less, Move More

There is no magic pill
If you want to live longer
and be healthy and trim
you must eat less
and go around
feeling deprived
so that even
if you don't live longer
it will seem longer

If you want to be healthy and trim
and live longer
you must exercise more
so even though
this may give you more years
they will be spent in the gym
and running on the track

Considering all the above
I will eat more, move less
and be happy

Eat Your Vegetables

When my children were little
I asked:
"Did you brush your teeth
put on sunscreen
clean up your room
finish your homework
and eat your vegetables?"

When they were older
I asked:
"Did you go to the doctor
pay all your bills
save for the future
put on sunscreen
and eat your vegetables?"

And when they are very old
I won't be there to ask:
"Did you put on sunscreen
and eat your vegetables?"

But they'll tell
their children
to do it

Present Tense Lacking

*I*n the first part of life
we make plans for the *future*
and hope to be happy then

In the last part of life
we remember the *past*
and having been happy then

We are lacking
the *present* tense

Work to Live
or Live to Work

*M*ost of us
after having
spent many years
working to live
spend many more years
living to work

And when finally
there is no more work
we don't know how to live

Making a Difference

Helping others
giving to others
being there for others

One hand extended
to touch another
one ear bent over
to hear the unspoken
eyes wide open
to see the unseen

A mouth whispering
a consolation
a heart willing
to soothe the pain
a mind ready
to solve a problem

Helping others
giving to others
being there for others
are also gifts
we give to ourselves

The Gifts
of Love

He Didn't Miss a Thing

If I go to some wonderful event
without my husband
I don't enjoy it
because he's not there to appreciate it, too

So when I'm alone
I must go only to events
I hope I won't like
in order to not sit all evening
regretting that he's not there with me

Then when I come home I can say
I'm so glad you did not come
You did not miss a thing

Teaching Love

We hug and kiss
when we're alone
If the children come in
we stop, embarrassed
We should hug and kiss
when the children are there
so that they can see
what love looks like

Dancing Lessons

We used to dance for fun
not knowing the right steps
but swaying with the music
our feet moving in rhythm

Then we took some dancing lessons
and now instead of moving
happily on the dance floor
doing our own invented steps
we try to count correctly
and argue whether
to turn right or left
We used to dance for fun
Now we stand paralyzed
on the dance floor
not knowing what steps to take
or where to place our feet

Since we are physically dyslexic
rhythmically challenged
and musically disadvantaged
we will return to dancing our way

The Scents of Life

The smell of pine needles
warmed by the sun
lying on the forest floor
The smell of a peach
bitten into
the juice running
down your hand
The smell of wild lilacs
that grow only
at upper elevations
The smell of the ocean
its seaweed
wet on the beach
The smell of a baby
as it goes to sleep
with a drop of milk
on its chin
The smell of bread baking
The smell of hot chocolate
The smell of a barbecue down the street
The smell of winter
The smell of summer
Your smell in bed
lying next to me

Time-Out

Busy all day
going from one thing to another
back to back without interruptions
Let's both stop I said
and have a cup of tea
What a good idea
was the reply
While waiting for
the water to boil
I looked in the fridge
and found some bagels
a piece of cheese
and a jar of plum jam —
part of a gift basket
from Christmas last
We sat at the dining-room table
with place mats and linen napkins
and slowly sipped our tea
I remembered my mother
putting jam in her teacup
I did the same
It's a Russian thing
We looked at the sky
Rain clouds were gathering
and the palm tree
outside our window
was beginning to rustle

We were quiet together
in the warmth of our room
relishing the gift
we had just given ourselves —
the gift of time-out
Let's do it more often

Reclaiming Us

$\mathcal{M}$ost often I respond
to the most pressing things
on my desk
on my e-mail
on my answering machine

Most often I accept invitations
to places I don't want to go
or with people I'm not that fond of

Most often I expect that I will always
have time for you at some later date
when it is more convenient

You were once my first priority
as I was once yours
We have allowed other people
and other events
to take our places

Knowing that time won't wait
that love won't wait
I hereby wish to reclaim you
and thus reclaim myself
not only to survive alone
but to live each day better with you
for when I do not choose you
I do not choose myself

The Crystal Ball

I look into the crystal ball —
the one my husband gave me many years ago
I look into it and see nothing
and so I wonder what the future will bring
There are many possible options
many different scenarios —
both of us getting older together
in our house on the hill
healthy and productive
with friends and family around
or living alone in a small apartment
or disabled in a skilled nursing facility

I look into the crystal ball
devoid of information
and wonder what joys and sorrows await us
We can bank on both for sure
It's the percentages that worry me
How much of each — joy and sorrow?
If I knew ahead of time
could I prevent the preventable
and better face the inevitable?
If I knew ahead of time
I would start worrying now
and so I look into that crystal ball
and am relieved that I see nothing

The Ties
That Bind

The umbilical cords that tied us
to our parents
are also those that forever bind us
to our children

As the children grow up
and go away from us
our relationships change
Although we interact as adults
we are never free of concern for them
and just as we are forever
"parental" to our children
we also remain "children"
to our aging parents
We are often surprised
to see ourselves revert
to old patterns of relating
we thought were shed
years ago

Forever Worrying

The minute my baby was born
I became vulnerable forever
I started worrying
whether he was gaining enough weight
When he was a child and got a fever
I worried about serious illness
When he was a teenager
I worried about car accidents
When he was in college
I worried about his making bad decisions
When he got a job
I worried about it being the right one
When he got married
I worried whether he'd be happy
When he became a father
I worried about the new baby
But when he called
and said he was worried
because I did not
answer the phone
right away
I knew I finally
had passed the torch

Phone Calls

The kids don't call
or if they do, it's not often enough
Old parents don't want to be
an interruption in their kids' busy lives
so they sit and wait for these phone calls

Or the opposite happens —

The kids call all the time
The daughter wants to share
her child's latest feat
The son has issues with his job
They call on Sunday and during the week
They call evenings and early mornings
while their elderly parents
are busy with their own lives
They call a lot
but it is a good thing
to have parents who are available
and children who care enough to call a lot
It is never too much
It is never too often
children calling their parents

It is a good thing
to be so connected
throughout our whole lives

Umbilical Cords

"A son is a son till he takes a wife —
a daughter's a daughter all of her life"

The umbilical cord with a son
gets neatly cut twice —
once when he's born
and then again when he leaves home
moves into his own place
gets a job, gets married

With a daughter
the umbilical cord is cut only once —
at birth —
and then stays connected
throughout a lifetime
In spite of her various attempts at stretching it
it never really breaks
It may have ragged edges
and be frayed and painful
but this umbilical cord
is like an endless
elastic band
strong enough
to encircle the earth

For no matter where
the daughter lives
she is only a phone call away
an e-mail, a letter
a connection to her mother
with a question
a story
or a sob
And when the mother is gone
the umbilical cord
stretches beyond the grave
to remind her forever
that it is still there

Unrealistic Expectations

*W*hen I was in my early twenties
giving birth to my babies
my mother was in her mid-forties
She came to help —
she cooked, she cleaned
and held the babies

My children were in their early forties
when giving birth to their babies
I was in my seventies
expected to cook and clean
and all I was good for
was holding babies

Grandchildren

*I*t is impossible to understand
the thrill of becoming a grandparent
unless that miracle has happened to you
I'm not particularly eager
to see photos of other people's grandchildren
but I know how excited
everyone will be to see mine

Baseball Fans

We went to the game
in the new ball park
specially built for our team —
my husband
my grandson
a friend and I

While the grandson
ate hot dogs and pizza
my husband kept explaining the game
to my friend and me
We chatted away
not watching the players
not understanding the plays
more interested
in each other's life stories

While fans were screaming
and waving their arms
we talked quietly
enjoying the happy mood all around us
feeling at once removed and involved
When we were told that we won
we joined in the celebration
shouting and waving our arms
It was a great game!

Best Friends

I have some friends I never see
who live thousands of miles away
We were best friends in college
or when our children were small

But now we call each other only
when we have good news
or when we're unhappy
or just need to reconnect

Neither the distance nor the years
seem to matter
We can start right up
where we left off
When there is no other way
good friends should be heard
if they can't be seen

Reflection

I passed by a storefront yesterday
and saw reflected in the glass
my mother

I startled and turned around
wondering what she was doing there
but it was me

Death of a Loved One

When someone
we have loved dies
it is as if a limb
has been taken away

When someone
we have loved dies
it leaves us limping
for a long time

When someone
we have loved dies
grief is a task
that must be undertaken
so healing can follow
and lead us to new
tomorrows

Forgetting

*W*hen you remember
something or someone
you resurrect that person or object
into a palpable image

When you forget
you cast a pall over that memory
and render people and things
into eternal oblivion
as if they had never been

Thus, forgetting
makes us destroyers
of our own past
obliterating events
as if they never happened
erasing people
and formerly beloved objects
as if they had never existed

Yet when we remember
something or someone
that person, object, or event
remains part of us —
an image that exists
for as long as we're alive

This Is
Progress?

To What End?

In spite of high-tech appliances
there is less leisure

In spite of affluence
there is greed

In spite of community
there is loneliness

In spite of medical advances
there is illness

In spite of progress
there is more stress

Since turning back the clock
will not help
turning it forward
will allow me to hope
for better times

The Latest Technology

I bought a new cell phone
with a camera
I read the manual very carefully
and still cannot figure out
which buttons to push
between options one and two
or how to save a picture
or delete it
I bought a new player
that has a DVD-R
and for the life of me
I cannot tell what I'm doing
Although I program
according to the directions
I keep getting football
instead of the movie
I so carefully picked

I have an old computer
It works fairly well
except for the occasional glitches
and the attachments that don't open
It's also quite slow
If I need help
I get to talk to a person
in Calcutta with a thick accent
who is difficult to understand
I am told to hit a button
that does not exist
on my keyboard
I'm afraid
to buy a new computer
and have to read a manual
the size of a novel
and still talk
to the man in Calcutta
or sometimes it's Mumbai
I am not looking forward
to the next generation of anything

Numbers

Numbers:
How tall is he?
How old are her kids?
How much do you weigh?

Numbers:
What is their combined income?
How many bedrooms do they have?
How many minutes do they exercise?
How many calories do you consume?

Numbers:
How fast does she type?
How many miles does he drive?
How many TVs are in their home?
What is your cholesterol level?

Numbers:
How long does it take?
How many times a day?
How often?
How much?

Numbers:
Obsessed by
Ruled by
Living by
Too many numbers!

Up and Down

Housing prices are too high
if you want to buy
but too low
if you want to sell

Everything is going up —
interest rates
gas prices
global temperatures
and blood pressure

Not enough is going down —
mortgages
stress levels
crime rates
and excess pounds

Consumerism

Because there is too much
of everything
there is not enough
of anything

Sitting

I get out of bed
to sit at the breakfast table
Then I sit at the computer
I sit in my chair
where I read
I sit at a meeting
at lunch, at the drive-through
I can sit on the lawn mower
in summer
or sit on the snow blower
in winter
instead of having to push them
The television has a remote
so I don't have to get up
to switch channels
After sitting at dinner
I sit through a movie
Then to bed
where I can finally
lie down
exhausted
from so much sitting
all day long

Do Not Disturb

We are living in a culture of youth worship
dominated by speed, immediacy, newness
control, competitiveness, profit
exaggeration, media blitz, variety
constant entertainment
We always want more
believing that we need more

We are living in a culture of wrong messages
instead of quiet
of attention to the details
of life's slower rhythms
of not marching to a different drum
but to the sound of a flute
to truth telling
to healing of self and others
to fewer possessions but more friends
fewer movies and more books
fewer restaurants
more eating at home
less television
more walks
silence
quiet and silence
peaceful
Shhhh...
Do not disturb

The Clock
of Life Is
Ticking

The Ball of String

I have a ball of string
Each inch is a day in my life
As it unwinds throughout the hours
I often wish it to go faster when I am ill
or eager for the next event
I also wish it would stop unwinding
when life is sweet
But my ball of string
has its own rhythm
and it gets smaller all the time
I do not know if it might break
I do not see the end of it
the last bit hidden in its center
But I do know
it will unravel all the way
until there is no more
And so I hold my ball of string
in my two hands
watching it slowly disappear
as each hour is going by
and when it's gone
so will I

Time Savers Are Killing Time

*D*igital watches
beepers
cell phones
phones on airplanes
faxes

Computers are
counting time
in nanoseconds

I carry around
my cell phone
and say to people
I meet
"Sorry, I gotta go..."
and rush off
trying to save time
in order to put it
in a savings account
that I will be able to dip into
someday when I have time

Except the savings account is empty
for all the time
has been used up
hurrying to save it

Compensations

Can't read the fine print
I'm losing my sight
Can't hear that high-pitched sound
I'm losing my hearing
Can't chew on that nut
I'm losing my teeth
Can't lift that heavy weight
I'm losing muscle mass
Can't take a chance on falling
I'm losing bone density
Can't make love all night
I'm losing my libido
Can't remember what you just said
I'm losing my mind

But —
I can read with glasses
I can hear with my hearing aid
I can chew with my new filling
I can lift weights in the gym
walk my dog every day
cuddle with my love
and ask you to repeat
what you just said

Preparation

I am always prepared

When I was seventy-nine
I would say
"By next year I will be eighty"
So when eighty came around
I said to myself
"What? Just eighty?"
It was old news and not a shock

What is still somewhat upsetting
is that I am at the beginning
of my ninth decade
That one does sound
outrageous!

Changing Times

While young children never have
enough of their parents
parents often have
too much of their young children

While parents never have
enough of their grown children
grown children often have
too much of their parents

We Need Younger Friends

We have many friends
in our own age group
In other words: seniors
One has arthritis and is in pain
One has frequent headaches
One has back problems
One can't see well
One can't hear
One limps
One is depressed
Our friends are getting older
and all complain
And as much as we are there
for all friends in times of need
we need to look for
younger people
with whom we'll talk
about fun things —
not our aches and pains

Rude Awakenings

I thought I was still a spring chicken
but my x-rays show compression of the spine
I thought I could run marathons
but my knees gave out on the way
I thought I could climb up the mountain
but I had to stop to catch my breath
I thought I could dance all evening
but I had to sit the next one out
I thought I could see forever
but I had to get bifocals
I thought my hearing was perfect
but people seem to mumble more
I thought I could learn new things quickly
but it takes me longer than before
I thought I could stay up all night
but I fell asleep on the living-room couch

I thought I was still a spring chicken
but I guess I'm just an old hen

Doing It Better!

The Pleasure Principle

The young are mostly driven
by the pursuit of pleasure
and the old by the avoidance of pain
Sadly, some of the young
are trying to avoid pain
but happily many of us old folks
are still just pursuing pleasure

Our Lives

Our lives are made up
of both the small, daily irritations
of unmet expectations
and the larger world issues

Laughing at some
talking about the others
may begin to make a difference

Acceptance

I need to learn tolerance
for the internal contradictions
and ambiguities
I need to accept that
thoughts and feelings are equally valid
I need to distinguish between
what others expect of me
and what I expect of myself
I don't need to respond to all requests
or conform to others' wishes
I must take into consideration
the difference between what I want
and what I need
and not confuse outside pressures
with inner priorities
The contradictions will always be there
I must accept them
as an inevitable part of my being
and not try to resolve them
as maturity finally takes hold
and wisdom does come
with age

My Bill of Rights

I have the right to
change my mind
make mistakes
cry or get angry
say "I don't know"
"I don't understand"
and "I don't care"
and offer no excuses
for my behavior

Something to
Look Forward To

*T*he way my life
is unfolding
I will probably have
an identity crisis
on my deathbed

Knock, Knock, Who's There?

Knock, knock
who's there
behind the wrinkles?

Knock, knock
who's there
under the white hair?

Who's there
with the slower step
a little bent over
pushing out of a chair?

Knock, knock
who's there
misplacing things
falling asleep
in front of the television
but wide awake
in the middle of the night?

Knock, knock
who's there
spoiling grandchildren
waiting for the kids to call?

Knock, knock
who's there?
We're there —
celebrating our lives
celebrating ourselves
wanting a better world
for our children
our grandchildren
wishing for peace

Knock, knock
who's there
behind the wrinkles
and under the white hair?
It's us... we're here

Tea Time

Sometimes at around 5 p.m.
I decide to skip dinner
and I put on my nightgown
get a tray
with a cup of tea
toast, and black cherry jam
and climb into bed
somehow feeling
deliciously decadent

At the Retirement Home

He comes in slowly
holding on to his walker
I'm glad to see him
still making it
to the dining room
for this will be me
if I live long enough

She sits with us at dinner
bubbling, chatting
about this and that
I think she's eighty
but she says she's ninety-eight
I want to be like her
when I grow up!

I prefer being a youngster
amongst my older peers
than the oldest
in a younger crowd
Few dye their hair here
No one talks of face-lifts
of Botox injections
or liposuction
We don't have to compete
Whatever way we look now
will have to do

We are all wearing out the clothes
we bought over a lifetime —
a jacket for Sunday brunch
and sensible shoes
so as not to trip and break a hip

We work out at the well-equipped gym
go to yoga and tai chi
do exercises in the pool
and join the walking group
We have a healthy salad for lunch
and always eat with friends
There are no lonely people here

We share our latest books
go to movies together
play bridge
attend weekly lectures on current events
music and art appreciation
A bus takes us to concerts and plays
We don't have to drive at night
The beauty salon is one floor down
The medical clinic is one floor up
The bank cashier comes twice a week

As I sit on my balcony
looking out over the endless ocean
with waves lapping a few feet below
I'm on a stationary cruise ship
sailing contentedly into my last years

There Is Always Chocolate

What is important?
Loving and being loved by my husband
my children and grandchildren
and having close friends
Doing work that I both value and enjoy
Being healthy
I like to be helpful to others
I like to write, walk on the beach with my dog
go to bed early and read
The usual things: music, theater
a good movie, dinner with friends
time alone with my husband
an e-mail from a grandchild
a sunny day, chocolate...
So far, so good —
I appreciate all the above every day
for inevitably some of it will disappear
because life has a way of crashing
into one's happiness
and obliterating it
sometimes in a matter of minutes
So in the meantime
I will make sure to eat enough chocolate

Today, All Is Well

Today, all is well
Tomorrow has no guarantees
but today the sun is shining
We got up
and nothing hurt

Today, all is well
The children are healthy
and have jobs
The grandchildren are
getting good grades
in high school and college

Today, all is well
We are sitting with good friends
not worried about the next meal
or where we will sleep tonight

Today, all is well
I don't know about tomorrow
so I stop whatever I'm doing
and appreciate the fact
that today all is well

About the Author

Natasha Josefowitz calls herself a late bloomer, having earned her master's degree at age forty and her PhD at age fifty. She was on the faculty of the business school at the University of New Hampshire and San Diego State University. She is a noted columnist and the author of seventeen books.

Dr. Josefowitz is an internationally known speaker, having lived and worked abroad and in the U.S. For ten years, she had her own weekly radio broadcast and a weekly television segment. Her efforts on behalf of women have earned her numerous awards, including *The Living Legacy Award* from the Women's International Center. She has been named *Woman of the Year* many times by various national and international organizations. She has been a guest on numerous television shows, including *Larry King Live* and *The Dr. Ruth Show*. Her articles have appeared in hundreds of magazines and journals, including the *Harvard Business Review*, the *Wall Street Journal*, the *London Times*, and *Psychology Today*. She currently writes a bimonthly column for the *La Jolla Village News* and for Jewishsightseeing.com.

Natasha has five children, ten grandchildren, and five great-grandchildren. She is white-haired, wrinkled, and has a couple of extra pounds, but she says she can celebrate life because she has PMZ (Post-Menopausal Zest).